why can't horses burp?

why can't horses burp?

Curious questions
about your favorite pet

Illustrated by Lily Snowden-Fine
Horse expert Dr. Nick Crumpton

Contents

History of the horse

How long have there been horses?

Horses didn't just appear overnight—they have evolved over the last 50 million years. By looking at fossil records we can retrace the history of the horse and see how it has changed over time.

Dawn horse

The earliest ancestral horses were the size of a dog, ate fruit and soft leaves in forests, and had four toes on each front foot and three on each back foot.

Horses and humans

We know that horses and humans met as early as 30,000 years ago because cave paintings of the animals from this time survive today.

Looking modern

Around 16 million years ago horses began to live on open grass plains. They grew larger teeth to chew the tough grasses and evolved to run fast to escape predators.

Family ties

Today, the horses' closest relatives are wild donkeys like the Asian kiang, domesticated donkeys and the zebras of Africa.

Fire and ice

Why are horses called warm-, hot- or cold-blooded?

Horse breeds are divided into three groups: warmbloods, hot bloods and cold bloods. These categories refer to their personalities and behavior, not body temperature.

Fiery fillies

Hot-blood breeds like the Lusitano were bred for speed and agility. They are high-spirited and energetic—which means they can be quite a handful for their human owners!

Steady stallions

Cold-blood breeds like Percherons are calm and intelligent, and were bred to pull carriages and help out on farms.

Mellow mares

Warmbloods like Haflingers aren't quite as laid back as cold bloods, but they are far less excitable than hot bloods.

They are calm and strong, as well as athletic and intelligent. They make great competition horses.

Wild stallions!

Do any horses still live in the wild?

Although most breeds of horse have been tamed by humans for hundreds of years now, sometimes a few escaped and began breeding in the wild. The descendants of these escapees are called "feral" horses and can be found all over the world today.

Northern lights

The small but muscular Icelandic horses spend half the year in the frosty highlands, so their thick, fluffy coats help protect them from the cold.

American idols

Mustang horses are descendants of the Spanish horses first brought to North America in the 16th century. Today, they are found in many states across the U.S.

Spirit of the past

The Przewalski's horse is actually a truly wild horse. Herds of them have lived in Mongolia for tens of thousands of years, and they remain the only horses never to have been domesticated.

Walkabout

Feral horses in Australia are called "brumbies." They live across the country and up in the Snowy Mountains in large herds called mobs or bands.

Dynamic duos

Can horses and humans be friends?

Horses are very social animals that like spending time with other horses and are often interested in meeting new animals—including humans. Some horse and human friendships that have formed over the years are particularly famous.

City horse

Bucephalus was the proud horse of Alexander the Great, the ancient ruler of the Greek Empire of Macedonia. Although Bucephalus was thought to be untameable, 12-year-old Alexander trained him and the two became inseparable. Alexander even founded the city Bucephala in his honor!

Rags to riches

Seabiscuit and his jockey John "Red" Pollard ran horse races in the 1930s. Both Seabiscuit and Pollard suffered injuries from accidents and everyone believed their racing careers were over, but after relearning how to walk together, they returned for one last race ... and shot to a triumphant victory in front of 78,000 fans!

Lights, camera, ACTION!

Trigger was a palomino horse who starred in many Wild West films in the 1930s to 1950s with his owner, Roy Rogers. Trigger knew 150 tricks and was even fully house-trained, so he was allowed into hospitals to cheer up sick children.

War horse

Marengo was the fearless Arabian war horse of Napoleon I of France. He was named after the Battle of Marengo, during which he heroically carried the French leader to safety.

13

Spot the difference

What color is that horse's coat?

Horses and ponies have pink or black skin, but their coats come in lots of different colors and markings, which can change as they grow older. The colors all have special names.

1. Piebald is a term used to describe a horse that is black with white splotches.

2. Bay horses are mostly brown with a black mane, tail and legs. It is one of the most common colors.

3. Chestnut horses have a reddish-ginger coat with a similar-colored mane and tail.

4. Strangely, white horses are actually called "**gray**." Horses with a gray circular pattern in their coats are called **dappled grays**.

14

5. Dun horses are a creamy color with a black mane and tail. Some have a dark stripe that runs right down the middle of their back, too.

6. Skewbald horses are white with different-colored patches (not just black).

8. Black horses are quite rare. They have a black coat with a black mane and tail.

9. Roans have a mix of white and colored hairs. Strawberry roans are pinkish and blue roans are a blue-silver.

7. Palomino horses have a golden-colored coat with a white mane and tail.

Built for speed

Can all horses be racehorses?

Not all horses are built for speed, but thoroughbreds are among the fastest in the world thanks to their extra-long legs, short backs and athletic build.

Origins of awesome

All thoroughbreds today are descendants of one of three great stallions: the Darley Arabian, the Godolphin Arabian and the Byerley Turk.

World domination

Thoroughbreds were first bred in England around 300 years ago. Today they are trained all over the world—from Japan to Switzerland—to compete in races.

Top speed

The fastest speed ever recorded was by thoroughbred filly Winning Brew, when she ran at a pace of 43.9 mph at the Penn National Race Course in Grantville, PA in 2008.

Coats of many colors

Although thoroughbreds are similar in shape to each other, they can be many different colors, such as black, chestnut or bay.

What's your neigh-m?

What are horses in a herd called?

Horses are very social animals that prefer living in groups called herds. To avoid squabbles, they have different roles. Humans have given them specific names...

A **stallion** is a large, muscular male horse over the age of four that protects other members of the herd from predators.

A **mare** is a female horse more than four years old. There may be many mares in a herd, but a herd will have one "lead mare."

A **filly** is a female horse that is less than four years old.

A **gelding** is a male horse that isn't able to father foals. Geldings usually make better riding or working horses due to their quieter temperaments.

A **colt** is a young male horse that is less than four years old. In the wild, colts leave and form a bachelor group until they are old enough to become the stallion in their own herd.

When colts and fillies are between one and two years old, they may be called **yearlings**.

A **foal** is a baby horse that is less than one year old. Foals are usually born at night and can stand up on their spindly legs as soon as an hour after birth.

Gentle giants

What are the biggest breeds of horse?

The largest breeds are called draft horses. These huge animals are very strong, and although they might look intimidating, are easygoing and relaxed when working with people.

A farmer's best friend

Before tractors were invented, Shire horses were used by farmers to pull heavy machinery. They were also used to tow barges along the many canals of Europe in the 19th century.

Super-sized stars

The Clydesdale horses that live near St. Louis, Missouri, are well-known for appearing in TV ads pulling wagons in a team of eight, accompanied by their Dalmatian sidekick.

Flares in the field

Draft horses have very large hooves. These help them to spread their weight on soft ground like muddy soil. They also have long hairs on their lower legs, known as feathering, to protect them from brambles.

Working nine to five

Do horses have jobs?

Ever since horses were first tamed, they have been helping humans by pulling carriages and towing heavy loads. Nowadays, machinery has replaced many of the jobs they once had, but horses still help people.

The long hooves of the law

In the U.S. and Canada, it takes a special horse to work with the mounted police. Just like police officers, police horses have to go through training and assessment to become part of the force.

A royal tradition

The British royal family use horse-drawn carriages on special occasions like royal weddings and birthdays. The horses are called "Windsor Grays" and are usually Irish Draft horses, chosen for the color of their coat and their calm nature.

Yee-haw!

Traveling hundreds of miles over the rocky American West might be difficult by car, but by horseback it is easy! Ranchers use strong stock horses like the American Quarter to keep cattle moving in the right direction.

23

Desert roots

Which is the oldest breed of horse?

We don't exactly know where and when horses were first tamed, but we do know that the Arabian horse was one of the first breeds to be domesticated. The Arabian horse was bred around 4,000 years ago by the nomadic Bedouin people of the Arabian Peninsula.

Desert rose

With their long, arched necks and their fine, silky manes and tails, Arabian horses are famous for their elegant looks.

Tough going

The Arabian horse was bred to travel long distances in the harsh desert heat during the day and the extreme cold at night.

Part of the family

Arabian horses were so prized by the Bedouin people that they were often brought into the family tent at night to protect them from bad weather, predators or thieves.

The long, the short and the tall

What's the difference between a horse and a pony?

Horses and ponies are the same species but they are given different names depending on their size. A pony is smaller than a horse and tends to have a very different personality too. But even though a pony is smaller, it is not a baby horse (that's a foal!).

A pony has a stocky skeleton that makes it very strong for its size.

A pony has a shaggy coat to keep it warm in cold weather.

A pony is often smarter than a horse. This means it can also be a bit naughtier!

A pony tends to live longer than a horse, and some can live to be over 30 years old.

A horse takes longer to reach its full height compared with a pony. It reaches its full size after six or seven years.

A horse has a shorter mane and a softer tail, and its hooves aren't as tough as a pony's.

A horse usually has a thinner coat, which means it might need a horse blanket to keep it warm in winter.

Because of its long legs, a horse can run faster than a pony.

A horse can eat twice as much hay as a pony and a lot more grain.

27

Fancy footwork

Can a horse perform tricks?

When we think of animals that can learn "tricks," we usually think of a dog rolling over or shaking a paw. The Lipizzaner is a very intelligent breed of horse that can be trained to perform much more complicated movements. At the Spanish Riding School in Vienna, riders train horses to hop, skip and jump.

Strength and beauty

Lipizzaners have very strong back legs. One of their famous dressage moves is the "levade," where the horse stands at a 30-degree angle. The "courbette" is where they hop on the spot on their back legs!

Going gray

Although Lipizzaners are recognizable for their snowy white coats, they are usually black when they are born and only begin to change to gray and white when they are around six years old.

Theme tunes
In the 1700s, the famous Austrian composer Wolfgang Amadeus Mozart wrote music for Lipizzaners to dance in time to at the "Grand Carousel" in Vienna.

Operation Cowboy
During World War II, the Lipizzaner stallions were evacuated out of Austria to protect them from bombs. They were safely returned to the Spanish Riding School after the war ended.

29

Looking good!

Do horses need a hairdresser?

In order to keep horses healthy and looking their best, it's important to groom them—especially as they love nothing better than rolling in a big puddle of mud to scratch any itches.

1. Loosen caked-on mud

The first step is to use the curry comb. Start from the ears and use small, circular motions over the coat to loosen and lift out any dirt. Be very careful around bony, sensitive areas like the legs.

2. Brush away loose hairs

Flick any dirt and loose hairs off the coat with a dandy brush. Don't use this brush on the horse's head or lower legs as these areas are sensitive.

3. Untangle longer hair

Manes and tails get knotted easily, but they can be untangled with a mane and tail comb. Make sure you stand to the side when combing the tail just in case the horse kicks!

4. Polish head to tail

Finally, use a softer body brush in long, smooth strokes from the head to the tail to get a clean, soft and shiny coat. This can also be used gently on the horse's face, ears and neck.

Healthy hooves

Why do horses wear shoes?

Domestic horses walk on soft surfaces, so their hooves don't become as thick as those of wild horses. This is why tame horses need to wear metal "shoes" to protect them. Keeping a horse's hooves and shoes in good condition is a very important job for its human owner.

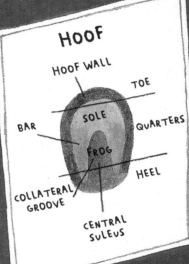

HOOF

HOOF WALL

TOE

BAR

SOLE

QUARTERS

FROG

HEEL

COLLATERAL GROOVE

CENTRAL SULCUS

What's in a toe?

Horse hooves are made from the same material as your fingernails and have three main parts. The "wall" or outer surface, the "sole" or main underside of the foot, and the "frog"—a special soft, bumpy area underneath the hoof that helps the horse grip the ground.

1. Removal and preparing

First, the farrier takes the old shoe off the horse's hoof. Then the hoof is cleaned, trimmed and the bottom is filed so that it is all level.

2. Picking out

Next the farrier uses a hoof pick to remove any dry dirt or manure stuck in the sole of the foot. "Picking out" should always be done very carefully as the frog is a sensitive area.

3. Forging and fitting

The farrier heats the metal shoe so that it can be hammered into shape on an anvil and, while the shoe is still hot, it is placed on the hoof to see how good a fit it is.

4. Nailing and finishing

When the farrier is happy with the shape and fit, the shoe is nailed into the hoof.*

*Don't worry! A hoof is dead material so having a shoe fitted doesn't hurt the horse.

33

Eating like a horse

How often should you feed your horse?

In the wild a horse can graze on grass and other edible shrubs and plants for up to 18 hours a day. Horses have quite small stomachs so it is important to feed your horse little and often, and always make sure it has time to digest it before exercise. Trotting with a bulging belly can be very uncomfortable!

Pick me ups

Some foods can help a horse stay in top shape. Eating linseed keeps the coat glossy, and mashed, warm bran is good for tired or sick horses.

Time for a treat

Apples, apricots and raisins are tasty treats and can be given as a reward when training.

Don't eat that!

Although grazing is a healthy way for horses to eat natural grasses, it is important they do not eat certain plants. Watch out for buttercups, acorns, ragwort, hemlock and foxgloves!

And don't eat too much!

Horses need to be careful early in the spring. Binge eating too much new, green grass (while very tasty) can make them seriously ill.

Why can't horses burp?

How is a horse unique?

In the wild, a horse spends most of its time on the move. It needs to keep a close eye out for any predators and be able to run away from them at any moment, even with a stomach full of food! A horse's body is specially designed to help do all these things.

The scoop on poop

An average horse can poop up to 13 times a day and can produce as much as 50 lb of manure. It's important to keep your horse's field tidy so you'd better be prepared to clean up a lot of mess!

On the look-out

Horses have eyes positioned on the sides of their heads, which means they can see nearly all the way around. This helps them to spot any predators that might sneak up from the side or slightly behind.

So why can't a horse burp?

The strong valves in a horse's stomach are designed to keep food in, even at a gallop. This means that a horse cannot burp or be sick!

Giddy up!

What is a horse gait?

Horses have distinct ways of moving at different speeds. As the horse runs faster, the pattern of its hooves hitting the ground changes.

These ways of walking and running are called gaits and are how a horse moves naturally rather than being taught by a trainer.

The **walk** is a horse's slowest gait. All four feet hit the ground one after another, so we say there are four "beats."

The **trot** is a slightly jumpier, faster gait, where the front foot and the opposite back foot come down at the same time, making two "beats."

The **canter** has three "beats," as one pair of feet hit the ground at the same time and the other two feet land one after the other.

The **gallop** is the fastest gait and contains four very quick "beats" as all the hooves hit the ground one after the other.

Horses can gallop at over 30 mph, but only for a short period of time.

Let the ears do the talking

Can a horse speak with its ears?

Horses have fantastic hearing. They can detect sounds as far away as 2.5 mi and can hear high-pitched noises better than humans. The ears are shaped like a funnel to channel noises to the eardrums and they can swivel them to focus on the direction from which the sound is coming. The position of a horse's ears will also tell you how it is feeling...

"Did someone just say my name?"

Horses can rotate their ears almost 180 degrees and move them one at a time. If one ear is pointing forwards and the other ear backwards, it is probably distracted!

"That looks cool"

When a horse's ears are pointing forwards, this means it is relaxed and interested in what is in front of it. If the ears are sharply angled forwards it might mean the horse is frightened of something.

"Stay away from me"

Look out! A horse with ears pinned back to its neck is angry and might kick or bite.

"Zzz...zzz"

This horse is very relaxed ... or even asleep! Be careful not to surprise a horse with its ears out to the side as it may be startled by you. Call its name first so it knows you're there.

"What was that noise?"

If the ears are turned— but not pinned—back, the horse is probably listening to something behind it. If it begins to swish its tail it might be getting a bit nervous.

"Who's there?"

If a horse's ears are flicking back and forth, this is a sign that it is feeling anxious and is trying to find out where a frightening noise or smell is coming from.

41

Competition time

Can a horse win a medal at the Olympic Games?

Horses competed in races in the Olympic Games in ancient Greece. They would pull chariots with their human drivers around laps of a stadium. Today, horses train together with their riders and compete in competitions for the gold, silver and bronze medals in three types of events.

Air show

Show-jumping courses test whether a horse and its rider can jump over 10–16 obstacles, each up to 6.5 ft—penalties are given if a horse refuses to jump one of the fences or if one is knocked down.

Prancing ponies

Dressage and para dressage are competitions where the horse and rider are judged on how gracefully they perform certain movements. It includes walking, trotting and cantering, and how well the horse responds to the rider's commands. It is sometimes thought of as "ballet on horseback."

Tournament time

Eventing takes place over three days and includes dressage, show jumping and a cross-country jumping phase. This requires the horse and rider to jump over as many as 40 outdoor obstacles over a four-mile-long course.

43

Glossary

Archaeologists – scientists and historians who study the ancient remains of humans and their cultures.

Anvil - a heavy iron block with a flat top on which metal can be hammered and shaped.

Bedouin – nomadic people who live in the Middle East and North African deserts.

Curry comb – a rubber or plastic brush used to loosen dirt in a horse's coat.

Dandy brush – a stiff brush used for removing dried mud from a horse's coat.

Digestion – when a person or animal's body breaks down food so it can use it for energy.

Domestication – when animals are tamed by humans and are able to be kept as pets or on farms.

Evolve – when the body parts of an animal or a plant slowly change over time.

Farrier – a person whose job involves taking care of horses' hooves, including making and fitting shoes for them.

Feathering – the long hair on the lower legs of some breeds of horses and ponies.

Forging – to make or shape a metal object by heating it in a fire and hammering it into shape.

Gait – the pattern of steps of a horse or another animal.

Grazing – feeding on grass on grasslands and prairies out in the open, rather than on plants under the cover of a forest.

Grooming – cleaning the coat of an animal by brushing it.

Herbivore – an animal that eats only plants.

Herd – a group of animals that live and feed together.

Predator – an animal that hunts and kills other animals for food.

Tame – an animal that is comfortable or relaxed in the presence of humans.

Index

First published in 2021 in the United States of America by
Thames & Hudson Inc., 500 Fifth Avenue, New York, New York 10110

Why Can't Horses Burp? © 2021 Thames & Hudson Ltd, London
Illustrations © 2021 Lily Snowden-Fine

Text by Nick Crumpton
Designed by Emily Sear

With special thanks to Jess Frith

Library of Congress Control Number 2020940128

ISBN 978-0-500-65230-5

Printed and bound in China by Shanghai Offset Printing Products Limited

Be the first to know about our new releases,
exclusive content and author events by visiting
thamesandhudson.com
thamesandhudsonusa.com
thamesandhudson.com.au

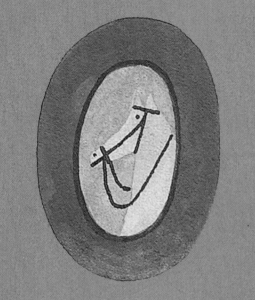